BRITISH
WARSHIPS
& AUXILIARIES

1990/91 Edition

C000147955

Price
£4.50

THE ROYAL NAVY

The numerical superiority of the NATO navies over those of the Soviet Union is claimed by Moscow to be a destabilising factor in the progress of reducing tension between East and West. Soviet leaders have hinted that they would like to see substantial reductions in the numbers of Western warships which they say are a threat to them.

But the whole fabric of Western society depends upon sea communications and thus the protection of those communications—the merchant ships of many nations. Their protection is not an option but a basic essential for the West. They are as vital to the preservation of the Western way of life as the KGB is to the Soviet form of society.

The Soviet Union and its allies have no such dependence upon shipping. Their troops in Eastern Europe can be reinforced, in hours, by train and road while trans-Atlantic reinforcement of the Allied forces in Europe would take weeks. If Moscow persists in its demands for comparable cuts in warship numbers by both NATO and the Warsaw Pact then the NATO nations should counter with a demand for the abolition of the KGB. Just as NATO's loss of control of the oceans would lead to its dismemberment and collapse so, too, would the disappearance of the KGB lead to fragmentation and winding up of much of the Soviet empire.

Forty-five years after the end of the Second World War Western political and military leaders are declaiming their belief that at last the Soviet Union wants to relax the tensions of the Cold War.

In the Soviet Union itself declining living standards coupled with growing revival of nationalism in several of the states and regions making up the USSR are seen in the West as almost certain to force the hand of the government in Moscow to put the needs of the consumer and civilian industry at the head of its list of priorities for the first time in over 70 years of "socialist achievement".

In some countries, significantly West Germany among them, Mr Gorbachev with his aims of re-forming and revitalising Soviet society is seemingly regarded as an equal if not a greater force for peace than President Bush.

Yet paradoxically, it is this same Mr Gorbachev who gave his personal approval to the construction of four new 80,000 ton Soviet aircraft carriers in addition to the four *Kiev* class ships already in service and two others of some 65,000 tons, one of which is probably named *Rossiya.* The existence of three of these latest 80,000 ton ships only became known to Western naval intelligence towards the end of 1989.

Also in the course of last year numbers of Soviet "Yankee" class nuclear ballistic missile submarines have been withdrawn from patrol areas in the Atlantic where their 1600 mile range missiles were targeted on cities in the eastern United States. To the alarm of some West European leaders, notably in Norway, it now appears that these submarines have patrol areas which would allow them to attack targets across most of Europe.

At least one "Yankee" has been refitted to launch the 2,200 mile range supersonic SS-NX-24 nuclear cruise missile. This weapon, which follows the contours of the earth over which it is flying, would be impossible for the Americans' Strategic Defence Initiative (SDI) system to detect since this is designed to detect and destroy ballistic missiles whose flight trajectory takes them outside the earth's atmosphere into space.

Though the SS-NX-24 is believed to be still under development another submarine launched nuclear cruise missile, the 1100 mile range SS-N-21, is already at sea in a very large number of Soviet nuclear submarines.

Cruise missiles are also operated by Soviet surface ships among them no doubt the new, very large, ship known to be under construction at Leningrad. At present it is not known if this is the fourth of the 28,000 ton *Kirov* class battlecruisers or a ship of a new design.

Earlier this year it did at least appear that the Soviet Navy was slackening the build up of its fleet with the apparent failure to start work on the seventh of the "Typhoon" class of 25,000 ton nuclear powered submarines armed with 20 4,500 mile range SS-N-20 "Sturgeon" nuclear ballistic missiles. But it now appears the delay with the latest boat was due to the slow rate of delivery of nuclear reactors—Soviet industry can, it seems, produce *only* 12 marine reactors a year. (Compared with perhaps one every 18 months in Britain!). But Mr Gorbachev's principal arms control advisor, Marshal Sergei Akhromeyev, former Chief of the Soviet General Staff, said earlier this year that in future all major Soviet warships would be nuclear powered.[1]

A naval programme of such magnitude, which also, of course, includes numbers of nuclear and conventionally powered attack submarines; destroyers; frigates and smaller warships and auxiliaries, hardly seems compatible with an avowed policy of reducing East-West tension, as Mr Gorbachev declares. Of course he can point to the US Navy's growing numbers of cruise missile armed ships but he has yet to show that the Soviet Union is prepared to match the reduction of one US carrier task group (that headed by the venerable carrier *Coral Sea*) and the sale and paying off during the next four years of some 42 US destroyers and frigates and with a further 47 frigates earmarked for part-manning by reservists as units of the Naval Reserve Force.

In a word, the US Navy's 600-ship fleet, planned in the early years of the Reagan administration, is no longer considered attainable in the near future. No comparable declaration of naval force reductions has yet come from Moscow.

Where, then, does this leave the Royal Navy for which further cuts in strength would raise serious doubts about its continuing credibility to conduct deep ocean operations?

Watching them watching us watching them . . .   ● OFFICIAL PHOTO

In a recent interview Admiral Sir Julian Oswald, the First Sea Lord, was quoted as saying that he genuinely believed the Soviets wished to see improvement in relations and a reduction in tension.[2]. "I think that means that our navy, while continuing to be sized, structured, trained and equipped for its NATO role, will be able to, and will be required by the government to, look rather more to out-of-area considerations". He cited interdiction of the drug trade as an example (which in the US is regarded by the public as a greater threat today to society than that posed by the Soviet Union according to a recent survey) and went on to say that: "Eventually, and it may not be far away, I believe we will see the structure of our forces moving towards more flexibility and more mobility to enable them to operate world-wide more effectively".

For some years now the RN's West Indies guardship has, when opportunity offers, been collaborating with US Coast Guard and other indigenous law enforcement agencies to counter the enormous flow of

5

drugs being smuggled into the United States from South America. Such activity has only recently been revealed because of Foreign Office fears that publicising the RN's operations might be considered a slight upon the anti-drug smuggling efforts of various small Caribbean states, mostly former British colonies.

This is but one example of the kind of activity the First Sea Lord probably had in mind. It is not difficult to look at the world map to identify other areas where law and order may break down to a point where the well-being of other peoples and nations are seriously threatened.

Though the Gulf war ended in 1988 issues between Iran and Iraq are by no·means resolved. Lying in the Italian shipyards where they were built, in some cases as long ago as 1985, are four frigates and six missile armed corvettes, worth around perhaps £1.5 billion, which Iraq is still unable to sail to their homeport. At some point a move will be made to get them home and this could signal a renewal of the conflict at least at sea.

In SE Asia the Vietnamese withdrawal from Kampuchea, formerly Cambodia, at the time of writing (October 1989) left grave fears that the reign of terror of the Chinese backed Khmer Rouge leader Pol Pot might begin again. Can the rest of the world really sit back and let a further two million or so people die in a renewal of the systematic butchery of 10 years ago? Today the nations of SE Asia are economically and militarily far stronger than they were in the 1970s and since Britain has defence obligations to two of them, (Malaysia and Singapore) the chances of at least a token British involvement in the area cannot be ruled out. China, Pol Pot's arms supplier and paymaster, last June demonstrated its own ruthlessness in suppressing student dissidents, which has not gone unnoticed by her Asian neighbours.

There remains also the Falklands issue and though the new Argentine government has disclaimed any intentions of retaking the islands by force, despite what was said during the election campaign in early 1989, it is taking steps to placate the military by ending show trials of officers accused of kidnapping, torture and murder of political opponents in the 1970s and early 1980s. It is probably going to be a very long time indeed before it is no longer necessary to have a permanent RN presence in the South Atlantic.

Another long-standing commitment for the RN is anti-gun running patrols around N. Ireland. It is, though, significant that the IRA has won something of a victory over the RN.

The aim of terrorists such as the IRA is to disrupt the society in which they operate to erode democratic processes and place restraints on the life of the individual. In this they have succeeded in that it now appears that the Defence Ministry's refusal to publish visits of HM Ships to UK ports far enough in advance to generate the level of interest the Navy needs to maintain its flow of recruits is based on the fear that too much notice might alert potential terrorists. Similarly, although the weekly CW List of RN officers' appointments was, with modifications, published throughout the Second World War it is no longer in public circulation because of the terrorist threat it is feared might arise if it were known

6

that Commander X were being appointed to the Ministry of Defence, from, say, command of a frigate. In the past the list was a fruitful source of "local boy" stories for weekly papers following the careers of native sons and daughters in the Service, thus further fostering the Navy's public image. Both these measures to curb publicity of the Service were put in hand during Mr Heseltine's time as Defence Secretary.

With manpower for ever concentrating the minds of senior officers in Whitehall these restrictions can only hinder the constant quest for more and more recruits. As more well qualified manpower is sought by the Royal Navy it now seems "highly likely" that an announcement will shortly be made offering girls a seagoing role in the Royal Navy. It will be interesting to watch the recruiting—and retention figures.

These various actual and potential troublespots, where it is conceivable the RN might at some point have to increase its presence, are vastly different to the North Atlantic war scenario which inevitably influences the design of many RN ships.

Frigates like the new Type 23 "Duke" class are designed to operate closely with supporting "one stop" Royal Fleet Auxiliaries, the new "Fort" class AORs—Auxiliary Oiler Replenishment—which will supply fuel as well as ammunition, food, spares and other "dry stores". But though the Type 23s' range of some 7,500 miles at 15 knots is considerably greater than that of preceding classes (the Type 22s have a range of 4,500 miles at 18 knots) their equipment is designed primarily to counter Soviet submarines of the latest types. Compared with some others these are fairly remote adversaries. The more likely problems the Type 23s may face are those such as high speed smugglers' or pirate craft against which towed array sonars or long range anti-ship missiles would play little part compared with, say, 20mm guns or helicopters or inflatables carrying armed boarding parties.

Twenty-five years ago in SE Asia during Indonesia's "Confrontation" campaign against Malaysia the RN acquired considerable experience in countering seaborne guerilla forces. The answer was not "County" class missile destroyers or *Whitby* class frigates, which formed the bulk of the Far East Fleet at the time, but constant patrolling by coastal minesweepers, seaward defence boats, and, inshore around Borneo, armed naval stores tenders and assault landing craft. Inconspicuous themselves these small warships, many of which were hurriedly brought forward from reserve with scratch crews, could watch for the craft whose course or speed among often hundreds of radar contacts and visual sightings aroused suspicion.

It is this kind of task, maybe conducted thousands of miles from the nearest shore support of any consequence, which seems the most probable scenario in which the RN is likely to operate in the 1990s. For such duties it is the patrol ship, such as the 10,000 mile range *Dumbarton Castle* and her sister ship *Leeds Castle*, which is likely to be much in demand; the more especially since these ships have a flight deck on which a Sea King helicopter can land. When ordered in 1980 it had been intended to build at least a further eight of these ships until the notorious

1981 Nott Defence Review bit deeply into the Navy's budget.

In 1983 a long-term possibility of ordering some patrol ships to supplement the Navy's frigates was publicly mentioned by the then Controller of the Navy, Admiral Sir Lindsay Bryson. In the intervening seven years no further mention has been made of such ships. In that time whatever funds have been made available for new ships have, rightly, concentrated on the construction of frigates, submarines and naval aircraft. But the time is fast approaching when the requirements for more general purpose light warships cannot be ignored. Some might combine at least the patrol task, such as with the Fishery Protection Squadron, with that of minesweeping—for which the Navy is still 20 ships short of its 1980 long term costing total of 50 by 1995.

Others, possibly a "repeat" of the *Castle* design, might combine the patrol task with minelaying and/or route surveillance in time of war or international tension using one of the remotely-operated sonar-equipped vehicles designed to enable large ships, warships and merchant ships, to avoid mines in their path.

At the other end of the scale the proposed new Aviation Support Ship, designed to carry around 15 troop-carrying helicopters and a Royal Marines Commando of some 750 men, must assume a greater priority than the leisurely pace of its development would so far indicate and the second ship of the type must become a firm project rather more than it is now. In "aid to the civil power" tasks, whether helping restore order or trying to make good the damage caused by earthquakes, hurricanes and the like, helicopters and the man with a rifle—or a pickaxe—is vital. As crews of RN frigates in the West Indies have demonstrated they can achieve much in helping the victims of natural disasters—but a frigate lacks the space to stow essential equipment and relief stores and has not got the manpower needed to cope with major disasters.

In a word it seems likely that the RN increasingly is going to return to a more far-ranging role in the world—something that was largely lost sight of in the swingeing cuts in the mid-1960s when it was decided there was no longer a call for anything other than a token RN presence, usually on an infrequent basis, outside the NATO area.

1. NAVINT 1/15 14 Aug 1989.
2. Jane's Defence Weekly 12/12 23 Sept 1989.

SHIPS OF THE ROYAL NAVY — PENNANT NUMBERS

Ship	Penn. No.	Ship	Penn. No.
Aircraft Carriers		CAMPBELTOWN	F86
INVINCIBLE	R05	CHATHAM	F87
ILLUSTRIOUS	R06	BROADSWORD	F88
ARK ROYAL	R07	BATTLEAXE	F89
		BRILLIANT	F90
Destroyers		BRAZEN	F91
BRISTOL	D23	BOXER	F92
BIRMINGHAM	D86	BEAVER	F93
NEWCASTLE	D87	BRAVE	F94
GLASGOW	D88	LONDON	F95
EXETER	D89	SHEFFIELD	F96
SOUTHAMPTON	D90	COVENTRY	F98
NOTTINGHAM	D91	CORNWALL	F99
LIVERPOOL	D92	PENELOPE	F127
MANCHESTER	D95	AMAZON	F169
GLOUCESTER	D96	ACTIVE	F171
EDINBURGH	D97	AMBUSCADE	F172
YORK	D98	ARROW	F173
CARDIFF	D108	ALACRITY	F174
		AVENGER	F185
Frigates		NORFOLK	F230
CLEOPATRA	F28	MARLBOROUGH	F231
SIRIUS	F40		
PHOEBE	F42	**Submarines**	
MINERVA	F45	ODIN	S10
DANAE	F47	OSIRIS	S13
JUNO	F52	ONSLAUGHT	S14
ARGONAUT	F56	OTTER	S15
ANDROMEDA	F57	ORACLE	S16
HERMIONE	F58	OCELOT	S17
JUPITER	F60	OTUS	S18
SCYLLA	F71	OPOSSUM	S19
ARIADNE	F72	OPPORTUNE	S20
CHARYBDIS	F75	ONYX	S21
CUMBERLAND	F85	RESOLUTION	S22

Ship	Penn. No.		
REPULSE	S23		
RENOWN	S26		
REVENGE	S27		
UPHOLDER	S41		
CHURCHILL	S46		
CONQUEROR	S48		
COURAGEOUS	S50		
TRENCHANT	S91		
TALENT	S92		
TRIUMPH	S93		
VALIANT	S102		
WARSPITE	S103		
SCEPTRE	S104		
SPARTAN	S105		
SPLENDID	S106	KELLIN	M1154
TRAFALGAR	S107	KIRKLIS	M1157
SOVEREIGN	S108	NURTON	M1166
SUPERB	S109	SHERATON	M1181
TURBULENT	S110	UPTON	M1187
TIRELESS	S117	SOBERTON	M1200
TORBAY	S118	SANDOWN	M101
SWIFTSURE	S126	WAVENEY	M2003
		CARRON	M2004
Assault Ships		DOVEY	M2005
FEARLESS	L10	HELFORD	M2006
INTREPID	L11	HUMBER	M2007
		BLACKWATER	M2008
Minesweepers		ITCHEN	M2009
& Minehunters		HELMSDALE	M2010
BRECON	M29	ORWELL	M2011
LEDBURY	M30	RIBBLE	M2012
CATTISTOCK	M31	SPEY	M2013
COTTESMORE	M32	ARUN	M2014
BROCKLESBY	M33		
MIDDLETON	M34	**Patrol Craft**	
DULVERTON	M35	PEACOCK	P239

Ship	Penn. No.	Ship	Penn. No.
PLOVER	P240	**Survey Ships & RN Manned Auxiliaries**	
STARLING	P241		
SENTINEL	P246	BRITANNIA	A00
CORMORANT	P256	GLEANER	A86
HART	P257	MANLY	A92
LEEDS CASTLE	P258	MENTOR	A94
REDPOLE	P259	MILBROOK	A97
KINGFISHER	P260	MESSINA	A107
CYGNET	P261	ROEBUCK	A130
PETEREL	P262	HECLA	A133
SANDPIPER	P263	HECATE	A137
ARCHER	P264	HERALD	A138
DUMBARTON CASTLE	P265	ENDURANCE	A171
		ETTRICK	A274
BITER	P270	ELSING	A277
SMITER	P272	IRONBRIDGE	A311
PURSUER	P273	BULLDOG	A317
ANGLESEY	P277	IXWORTH	A318
ALDERNEY	P278	BEAGLE	A319
BLAZER	P279	FAWN	A335
DASHER	P280	DATCHET	A357
ATTACKER	P281	CHALLENGER	K07
CHASER	P282		
FENCER	P283		
HUNTER	P284		
STRIKER	P285		
PUNCHER	P291	This book is updated and re-issued every *December.* Keep up to date . . . Don't miss the new edition. Phone 0579 43663 for details.	
CHARGER	P292		
RANGER	P293		
TRUMPETER	P294		
JERSEY	P295		
GUERNSEY	P297		
SHETLAND	P298		
ORKNEY	P299		
LINDISFARNE	P300		

● HMS NEPTUNE

HMS Renown

RESOLUTION CLASS

Ship	Pennant Number	Completion Date	Builder
RESOLUTION	S22	1967	Vickers
REPULSE	S23	1968	Vickers
RENOWN	S26	1968	C. Laird
REVENGE	S27	1969	C. Laird

Displacement 8,400 tons (submerged) **Dimensions** 130m x 10m x 9m **Speed** 25 knots **Armament** 16 Polaris Missiles, 6 Torpedo Tubes **Complement** 147 (x 2).

Notes

These four nuclear-powered Polaris submarines are the United Kingdom's contribution to NATO's strategic nuclear deterrent. At least one of them is constantly on patrol and because of their high speed, long endurance underwater, and advanced sonar and electronic equipment they have little fear of detection.

Each submarine carries 16 Polaris two-stage ballistic missiles, powered by solid fuel rocket motors, 9.45 metres long, 1.37 metres diameter and weighing 12,700 kilogrammes with a range of 2,500 miles. The first of a new Vanguard Class was laid down in December 1986 and the second ordered in October 1987. They will carry the Trident D5 missile with a range of up to 6,000 miles. The first ship of the class (Vanguard), is not expected to enter service until 1994.

● HMS NEPTUNE

HMS Courageous

VALIANT CLASS

Ship	Pennant Number	Completion Date	Builder
CHURCHILL	S46	1970	Vickers
CONQUEROR	S48	1971	C. Laird
COURAGEOUS	S50	1971	Vickers
VALIANT	S102	1966	Vickers
WARSPITE	S103	1967	Vickers

Displacement 4,900 tons dived **Dimensions** 87m x 10m x 8m **Speed** 28 knots + **Armament** 6 Torpedo Tubes **Complement** 103.

Notes
DREADNOUGHT—the forerunner of this class—is awaiting disposal (by scrap or sinking) at Rosyth. These boats are capable of high underwater speeds and can remain on patrol almost indefinitely. They are able to circumnavigate the world without surfacing. Cost £24-£30 million each to build. Refit and maintenance periods for these boats are becoming longer as the class begins to age.

SUBMARINES

● HMS NEPTUNE

HMS Superb

SWIFTSURE CLASS

Ship	Pennant Number	Completion Date	Builder
SCEPTRE	S104	1978	Vickers
SPARTAN	S105	1979	Vickers
SPLENDID	S106	1980	Vickers
SOVEREIGN	S108	1974	Vickers
SUPERB	S109	1976	Vickers
SWIFTSURE	S126	1973	Vickers

Displacement 4,500 tons dived **Dimensions** 83m x 10m x 8m **Speed** 30 knots + dived **Armament** 5 Torpedo Tubes **Complement** 116.

Notes
A follow-on class of ships from the successful Valiant Class. These submarines have an updated Sonar and Torpedo system. The class is transferring base port from Devonport to Faslane.

14

HMS Trafalgar

TRAFALGAR CLASS

Ship	Pennant Number	Completion Date	Builder
TRENCHANT	S91	1989	Vickers
TRAFALGAR	S107	1983	Vickers
TURBULENT	S110	1984	Vickers
TIRELESS	S117	1985	Vickers
TORBAY	S118	1986	Vickers
TALENT	S92	1990	Vickers
TRIUMPH	S93	1991	Vickers

Displacement 4,500 tons **Dimensions** 85m x 10m x 8m **Speed** 30 + dived **Armament** 5 Torpedo Tubes **Complement** 125.

Notes
Enhanced development of the Swiftsure Class. Quieter, faster and with greater endurance than their predecessors. Design work for a follow on ('W' class) is in progress, but orders are unlikely before 1993.

15

● VSEL

HMS Upholder

UPHOLDER CLASS

Ship	Pennant Number	Completion Date	Builder
UPHOLDER	S41	1989	Vickers
UNSEEN	S42		Cammel Laird
URSULA	S43		Cammel Laird
UNICORN	S44		Cammel Laird

Displacement 2,400 tons **Dimensions** 70m x 8m x 5m **Speed** 20 knots Dived **Armament** 6 Torpedo Tubes: Sub Harpoon missile **Complement** 44.

Notes

A new class of (possibly 19) conventionally powered submarines. UPHOLDER'S entry into service has been delayed by industrial disputes and trials problems, and the building of her sister ships slowed down until these problems are rectified.

16

HMS Opportune

OBERON CLASS

Ship	Pennant Number	Completion Date	Builder
ODIN	S10	1962	C. Laird
OSIRIS	S13	1964	Vickers
ONSLAUGHT	S14	1962	Chatham D'yard
OTTER	S15	1962	Scotts
ORACLE	S16	1963	C. Laird
OCELOT	S17	1964	Chatham D'yard
OTUS	S18	1963	Scotts
OPOSSUM	S19	1964	C. Laird
OPPORTUNE	S20	1964	Scotts
ONYX	S21	1967	C. Laird

Displacement 2,410 tons (submerged) **Dimensions** 90m x 8m x 5m **Speed** 12 knots surface, 17 knots submerged **Armament** 8 Torpedo Tubes **Complement** 70.

Notes
Service lives of most hulls are being extended due to the slow rate of ordering for the replacement Upholder class. OLYMPUS sold to Canada in 1989 for use as a static harbour training vessel. Some vessels to be sold to Egypt at the end of their RN service.

HMS Invincible

INVINCIBLE CLASS

Ship	Pennant Number	Completion Date	Builder
INVINCIBLE	R05	1979	Vickers
ILLUSTRIOUS	R06	1982	Swan-Hunter
ARK ROYAL	R07	1985	Swan-Hunter

Displacement 19,500 tons **Dimensions** 206m x 32m x 6.5m **Speed** 28 knots **Armament** Sea Dart Missile, 2 x 20mm guns, 3 Phalanx/Goalkeeper **Aircraft** 8 x Sea Harrier, 12 x Sea King **Complement** 900 + aircrews.

Notes
Manpower problems dictate that two ships are kept in the operational fleet, with the third being in refit or reserve. INVINCIBLE rejoined the fleet after refit in 1989, replacing ILLUSTRIOUS. The latter being placed in reserve (at Portsmouth) prior to refitting in 1991.

HMS Intrepid

FEARLESS CLASS

Ship	Pennant Number	Completion Date	Builder
FEARLESS	L10	1965	Harland & Wolff
INTREPID	L11	1967	J. Brown

Displacement 12,500 tons, 19,500 tons(flooded) **Dimensions** 158m x 24m x 8m **Speed** 20 knots **Armament** 2 Sea Cat Missile Systems, 2 x 40mm guns, 4 x 30mm + 2 x 20mm (INTREPID only). **Complement** 580.

Notes
Multi-purpose ships that can operate helicopters for embarked Royal Marine Commandos. 4 landing craft are carried on an internal deck and are flooded out when the ship docks down. One ship is usually in refit or reserve—FEARLESS will replace INTREPID as the operational vessel during 1990. An order for a new Aviation Support Ship is expected to be placed in 1990.

19

AIRCRAFT CARRIERS

ASSAULT SHIPS

HMS Bristol

BRISTOL CLASS (Type 82)

Ship	Pennant Number	Completion Date	Builder
BRISTOL	D23	1972	Swan Hunter

Displacement 6,750 tons **Dimensions** 154m x 17m x 7m **Speed** 30 knots + **Armament** 1 x 4.5″ gun, 1 Sea Dart Missile System, 4 x 30mm + 4 x 20mm guns **Complement** 407.

Notes
Four ships of this class were ordered but three later cancelled when requirement for large escorts for fixed wing aircraft carriers ceased to exist. Helicopter Deck provided but no aircraft normally carried. Fitted for, but not with, Vulcan Phalanx. Frequently employed as the Dartmouth Training ship for young officers.

20

HMS Exeter

SHEFFIELD CLASS
(Type 42) Batch 1 & 2

Ship	Pennant Number	Completion Date	Builder
BIRMINGHAM	D86	1976	C. Laird
NEWCASTLE	D87	1978	Swan Hunter
GLASGOW	D88	1978	Swan Hunter
EXETER	D89	1980	Swan Hunter
SOUTHAMPTON	D90	1981	Vosper T.
NOTTINGHAM	D91	1982	Vosper T.
LIVERPOOL	D92	1982	C. Laird
CARDIFF	D108	1979	Vickers

Displacement 3,660 tons **Dimensions** 125m x 15m x 7m **Speed** 29 knots **Armament** 1 x 4.5″ gun, 4 x 20mm guns, Sea Dart Missile System: 2 x Phalanx, Lynx Helicopter. 6 Torpedo Tubes **Complement** 280 +.

Notes
Sister ships SHEFFIELD and COVENTRY lost in 1982 during the Falklands conflict. All ships are to be modernised with new radar and electronic warfare systems. SOUTHAMPTON under repair (cost approx £45 million) throughout 1990 after collision in the Gulf (Sept 1988).

HMS Edinburgh

SHEFFIELD CLASS
(Type 42) (Batch 3)

Ship	Pennant Number	Completion Date	Builder
MANCHESTER	D95	1983	Vickers
GLOUCESTER	D96	1984	Vosper T.
EDINBURGH	D97	1985	C. Laird
YORK	D98	1984	Swan Hunter

Displacement 4,775 tons **Dimensions** 132m x 15m x 7m **Speed** 30 knots + **Armament** 1 x 4.5″ gun, 2 x Phalanx, 4 x 20mm guns Sea Dart missile system. Lynx helicopter, 6 Torpedo Tubes **Complement** 301.

Notes
"Stretched" versions of earlier ships of this class. Designed to provide area defence of a task force. Deck edge stiffening being fitted to counter increased hull stress. Lightweight Seawolf will be fitted from 1991. No Phalanx in EDINBURGH. The NFR90 (Nato Standard Frigate) was being studied as a possible replacement for these ships but since the UK participation cancelled (late 1989) studies for a different (UK) design are urgently being considered.

● HMS OSPREY

HMS Brazen

BROADSWORD CLASS
(Type 22) (Batch 1)

Ship	Pennant Number	Completion Date	Builder
BROADSWORD	F88	1978	Yarrow
BATTLEAXE	F89	1980	Yarrow
BRILLIANT	F90	1981	Yarrow
BRAZEN	F91	1982	Yarrow

Displacement 3,860 tons **Dimensions** 131m x 15m x 6m **Speed** 29 knots **Armament** 4 Exocet Missiles, 2 Sea Wolf Missile Systems, 4 x 30mm guns, 2 or 4 x 20mm guns, 6 Torpedo Tubes, 2 Lynx Helicopters **Complement** 224.

Notes
Planned successor to the Leander Class. Although capable of carrying 2 helicopters, only 1 normally embarked.

FRIGATES

HMS London

BROADSWORD CLASS
(Type 22) (Batch 2)

Ship	Pennant Number	Completion Date	Builder
BOXER	F92	1983	Yarrow
BEAVER	F93	1984	Yarrow
BRAVE ●	F94	1985	Yarrow
LONDON ●	F95	1986	Yarrow
SHEFFIELD ●	F96	1987	Swan Hunter
COVENTRY ●	F98	1988	Swan Hunter

Displacement 4100 tons **Dimensions** 143m x 15m x 6m **Speed** 30 knots **Armament** 4 Exocet Missiles, 2 Sea Wolf Missile Systems, 4 x 30mm + 2 x 20mm guns, 6 Torpedo Tubes, 2 Lynx Helicopters **Complement** 273.

Notes
● Ships have enlarged hanger and flight deck. Can carry SeaKing helicopter if required, and eventually, the EH101 (Merlin).

G. DAVIES

HMS Campbeltown

BROADSWORD CLASS
(Type 22) (Batch 3)

Ship	Pennant Number	Completion Date	Builder
CUMBERLAND	F85	1988	Yarrow
CAMPBELTOWN	F86	1988	C. Laird
CHATHAM	F87	1989	Swan Hunter
CORNWALL	F99	1987	Yarrow

Displacement 4,200 tons **Dimensions** 147m x 15m x 7m **Speed** 30 knots **Armament** 1 x 4.5″ gun, 1 x Goalkeeper, 8 Harpoon, Seawolf, 4 x 30mm guns, 6 Torpedo Tubes, 2 Lynx or 1 Sea King helicopter **Complement** 250.

Notes
General purpose gun and Goalkeeper system added to these ships as a direct result of lessons learned during Falklands conflict. All these ships have a major A/S and intelligence gathering capability. Cost £180 million each.

25

● L/AIR P. BALL

HMS Norfolk

DUKE CLASS (Type 23)

Ship	Pennant Number	Completion Date	Builder
NORFOLK	F230	1989	Yarrow
MARLBOROUGH	F231	Building	Swan Hunter
ARGYLL	F232	Building	Yarrow
LANCASTER	F233	Building	Yarrow
IRON DUKE	F234		Yarrow
MONMOUTH	F235		Yarrow
MONTROSE	F236		Yarrow

Displacement 3,500 tons **Dimensions** 133m x 15m x 5m **Speed** 28 knots **Armament** Harpoon & Seawolf missile systems: 1 x 4.5″ gun, 4 x 2 twin, magazine launched, Torpedo Tubes **Complement** 157.

HMS Juno

LEANDER CLASS

Ship	Pennant Number	Completion Date	Builder
JUNO	F52	1967	Thornycroft
ARIADNE	F72	1972	Yarrow

Displacement 2,962 tons **Dimensions** 113m x 13m x 5m **Speed** 27 knots **Armament** 2 x 4.5″ guns, 3 x 20mm guns, 1 Sea Cat Missile system, 1 Mortar Mk10, **Complement** 260.

Notes
JUNO (with a much reduced armament) is a training ship. ACHILLES paid off in 1989 (for sale). ARIADNE is due for disposal during 1990. She is the last steam propelled surface warship to be built for the Royal Navy. No Ikara Leanders remain in service. NAIAD (hulk) has a static trials role at Portsmouth/Rosyth.

HMS Hermione

LEANDER CLASS
(Sea Wolf Conversions)

Ship	Pennant Number	Completion Date	Builder
ANDROMEDA	F57	1968	HM Dockyard Portsmouth
HERMIONE	F58	1969	Stephen
JUPITER	F60	1969	Yarrow
SCYLLA	F71	1970	HM Dockyard Devonport
CHARYBDIS	F75	1969	Harland & Wolff

Displacement 2,962 tons **Dimensions** 113m x 13m x 5m **Speed** 27 knots **Armament** Sea Wolf System, 4 x Exocet Missiles, 2 x 20mm guns, 6TT, 1 Lynx helicopter **Complement** 260.

Notes
The refitting of these ships cost in the region of £70m—ten times their original cost—but modernisation programme curtailed from 10 to 5 ships. They are now packed with the latest anti-submarine technology. Small calibre armaments vary between individual ships.

28

● HMS OSPREY

HMS Cleopatra

LEANDER CLASS
(Exocet Conversions)

Ship	Pennant Number	Completion Date	Builder
● CLEOPATRA	F28	1966	HMD Devonport
● SIRIUS	F40	1966	HMD Portsmouth
● PHOEBE	F42	1966	Stephens
MINERVA	F45	1966	Vickers
DANAE	F47	1967	HMD Devonport
● ARGONAUT	F56	1967	Hawthorn Leslie
PENELOPE	F127	1963	Vickers

Displacement 2,860 tons **Dimensions** 113m x 12m x 5m **Speed** 27 knots **Armament** 4 Exocet Missiles, 3 Sea Cat Missile Systems, 2 x 40mm guns, 6 Torpedo Tubes, 1 Lynx helicopter **Complement** 230.

Notes
● Ships have been refitted with Towed Array sonar and their armament reduced to 2 Sea Cat systems. The 20mm guns replaced 40mm weapons to reduce top weight. Structural and mechanical problems are increasing the maintenance requirement for these elderly Leander class ships, but they have given excellent service during their long careers.

HMS Amazon

AMAZON CLASS (Type 21)

Ship	Pennant Number	Completion Date	Builder
AMAZON	F169	1974	Vosper T.
ACTIVE	F171	1977	Vosper T.
AMBUSCADE	F172	1975	Yarrow
ARROW	F173	1976	Yarrow
ALACRITY	F174	1977	Yarrow
AVENGER	F185	1978	Yarrow

Displacement 3,250 tons **Dimensions** 117m x 13m x 6m **Speed** 30 knots **Armament** 1 x 4.5″ gun, 2 x 20mm guns, 4 Exocet Missiles, 1 Sea Cat Missile System, 1 Lynx helicopter, 6 Torpedo Tubes **Complement** 170.

Notes

Sister ships ANTELOPE and ARDENT lost during the Falklands conflict. All 6 ships have been given extra hull strengthening. This class (built to a commercial design, and subsequently sold to the Ministry of Defence) have received no major mid-life modernisation but continue to play a first class general purpose role in the fleet.

HMS Hurworth

MINE COUNTERMEASURES SHIPS (MCMV'S) BRECON CLASS

Ship	Completion Date	Pennant Number	Builder
BRECON	1980	M29	Vosper T.
LEDBURY	1981	M30	Vosper T.
CATTISTOCK	1982	M31	Vosper T.
COTTESMORE	1983	M32	Yarrow
BROCKLESBY	1983	M33	Vosper T.
MIDDLETON	1984	M34	Yarrow
DULVERTON	1983	M35	Vosper T.
BICESTER	1986	M36	Vosper T.
CHIDDINGFOLD	1984	M37	Vosper T.
ATHERSTONE	1987	M38	Vosper T.
HURWORTH	1985	M39	Vosper T.
BERKELEY	1988	M40	Vosper T.
QUORN	1989	M41	Vosper T.

Displacement 625 tonnes **Dimensions** 60m x 10m x 2.2m **Speed** 17 knots **Armament** 1 x 30mm + 2 x 20mm guns **Complement** 45.

Notes

The largest warships ever built of glass reinforced plastic. Designed to replace the Coniston Class—their cost (£35m each) has dictated the size of the class. Very sophisticated ships—and lively seaboats! Some ships still equipped with 40mm weapons.

G. DAVIES

HMS Helmsdale

FLEET MINESWEEPERS
RIVER CLASS

Ship	Pennant Number	Completion Date	Builder
WAVENEY	M2003	1984	Richards
CARRON	M2004	1984	Richards
DOVEY	M2005	1984	Richards
HELFORD	M2006	1984	Richards
HUMBER	M2007	1985	Richards
BLACKWATER	M2008	1985	Richards
ITCHEN	M2009	1985	Richards
HELMSDALE	M2010	1985	Richards
ORWELL	M2011	1985	Richards
RIBBLE	M2012	1985	Richards
SPEY	M2013	1985	Richards
ARUN	M2014	1986	Richards

Displacement 850 tons **Dimensions** 47m x 10m x 3m **Speed** 14 knots **Armament** 1 x 40mm, 2 x GPMG **Complement** 30.

Notes

Built as replacements for the MCM ships serving with the RNR. BLACKWATER has an RN ships company and is in the Fishery Protection Squadron (FPS). Built to commercial specifications with steel hulls. Designed for 'sweeping in deep water. Orders for four more of this class were expected in 1987 but are still not forthcoming. Older Coniston class retained in service until new vessels ordered—or tasks reduced.

32

G. DAVIES

HMS Brereton

CONISTON CLASS

Ship	Penn. No.	Ship	Penn. No.
BRERETON (H)	M1113	KELLINGTON (H)	M1154
BRINTON (H)	M1114	KIRKLISTON (H) ●	M1157
WILTON (H)	M1116	NURTON (H)	M1166
CUXTON (S)	M1125	SHERATON (H)	M1181
GAVINTON (H) ●	M1140	§UPTON (S)	M1187
HUBBERSTON (H)	M1147	§SOBERTON (S)	M1200
IVESTON (H)	M1151	● In Reserve at Portsmouth	
KEDLESTON (H)	M1153		

Displacement 425 tons **Dimensions** 46m x 9m x 3m **Speed** 15 knots **Armament** 1 x 40mm gun, **Complement** 29/38.

Notes

120 of this class were built in the early 50s but most have now been sold overseas or scrapped. They have fulfilled many roles over the years and have given excellent service. WILTON, built of glassfibre in 1973, was the world's first 'plastic' warship. Ships marked § are employed on Coastal Fishery Protection duties. Ships marked (S) are Minesweepers—(H) Minehunters.

G. DAVIES

HMS Sandown

SANDOWN CLASS

Ship	Pennant Number	Completion Date	Builder
SANDOWN	M101	1989	Vosper T.
INVERNESS	M102		Vosper T.
CROMER	M103		Vosper T.
WALNEY	M104		Vosper T.
BRIDPORT	M105		Vosper T.

Displacement 450 tons **Dimensions** 53m x 10m x 2m **Speed** 13 knots **Armament** 1 x 30mm gun **Complement** 34.

Notes
A new class dedicated to a single mine hunting role. Propulsion is by vectored thrust and bow thrusters. Up to 15 more ships are envisaged. Six similar ships are being built for Saudi Arabia.

● OFFICIAL PHOTO

HMS Leeds Castle

CASTLE CLASS

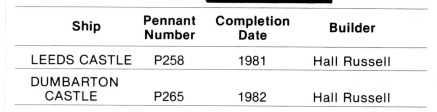

Ship	Pennant Number	Completion Date	Builder
LEEDS CASTLE	P258	1981	Hall Russell
DUMBARTON CASTLE	P265	1982	Hall Russell

Displacement 1,450 tons **Dimensions** 81m x 11m x 3m **Speed** 20 knots **Armament** 1 x 40mm gun **Complement** 40.

Notes

These ships have a dual role—that of fishery protection and off-shore patrols within the limits of UK territorial waters. Unlike the Island Class these ships are able to operate helicopters—including Sea King aircraft. Trials have been conducted to assess the suitability of these ships as Minelayers. LEEDS CASTLE currently on long term deployment to the Falklands Islands with ships companies rotating every four months.

35

HMS Lindisfarne

ISLAND CLASS

Ship	Pennant Number	Completion Date	Builder
ANGLESEY	P277	1979	Hall Russell
ALDERNEY	P278	1979	Hall Russell
JERSEY	P295	1976	Hall Russell
GUERNSEY	P297	1977	Hall Russell
SHETLAND	P298	1977	Hall Russell
ORKNEY	P299	1977	Hall Russell
LINDISFARNE	P300	1978	Hall Russell

Displacement 1,250 tons **Dimensions** 60m x 11m x 4m **Speed** 17 knots **Armament** 1 x 40mm gun **Complement** 39.

Notes
Built on trawler lines these ships were introduced to protect the extensive British interests in North Sea oil installations and to patrol the 200 mile fishery limit.

HMS Plover

PEACOCK CLASS

Ship	Pennant Number	Completion Date	Builder
PEACOCK	P239	1983	Hall Russell
PLOVER	P240	1983	Hall Russell
STARLING	P241	1984	Hall Russell

Displacement 700 tons **Dimensions** 60m x 10m x 5m **Speed** 28 knots **Armament** 1 x 76mm gun **Complement** 31.

Notes

The first warships to carry the 76mm Oto Melara gun. They are used to provide an ocean going back-up to the Marine Department of the Hong Kong Police. The Government of Hong Kong has paid 75% of the building and maintenance costs of these vessels. Sister ships SWALLOW and SWIFT returned to UK in 1988 and were sold (Oct 88) to the Irish Navy after only 3 years RN service.

37

HMS NEPTUNE

SENTINEL CLASS

Ship	Pennant Number	Completion Date	Builder
SENTINEL	P246	1975	Husumwerft

Displacement 1710 tons **Dimensions** 60m x 13m x 4m **Speed** 14 knots **Armament** 2 x 40mm **Complement** 26.

Notes
Formerly the Oil Rig support vessel Seaforth Saga. Employed in the Clyde area on Submarine escort duties—and "marking" of Soviet vessels off N. Ireland.

M. LOUAGIE

HMS Dasher

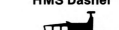

COASTAL TRAINING CRAFT
ARCHER CLASS

Displacement 43 tonnes **Dimensions** 20m x 6m x 1m **Speed** 20 knots **Armament** Nil **Complement** 14

Ship	Pennant Number	Completion Date	Builder
ARCHER	P264	1985	Watercraft
BITER	P270	1985	Watercraft
SMITER	P272	1986	Watercraft
PURSUER	P273	1988	Vosper
BLAZER	P279	1988	Vosper
DASHER	P280	1988	Vosper
PUNCHER	P291	1988	Vosper
CHARGER	P292	1988	Vosper
RANGER	P293	1988	Vosper
TRUMPETER	P294	1988	Vosper

Notes
In service with RNR divisions and RN University units.

39

HMS Hart

BIRD CLASS

Ship	Pennant Number	Completion Date	Builder
CORMORANT	P256	1976	James & Stone
HART	P257	1976	James & Stone
REDPOLE	P259	1970	Fairmile
KINGFISHER	P260	1975	R. Dunston
CYGNET	P261	1976	R. Dunston
PETEREL	P262	1976	R. Dunston
SANDPIPER	P263	1977	R. Dunston

Displacement 190 tons **Dimensions** 37m x 7m x 2m **Speed** 21 knots **Complement** 24.

Notes

PETEREL and SANDPIPER are training ships attached to the Britannia Royal Naval College at Dartmouth. REDPOLE, HART and CORMORANT commissioned into the Royal Navy in 1985 after service as RAF search and rescue craft. HART & CORMORANT are smaller craft and are based at Gibraltar.

40

HMS Hunter

ATTACKER CLASS

Ship	Pennant Number	Completion Date	Builder
ATTACKER	P281	1983	Allday
CHASER	P282	1984	Allday
FENCER	P283	1983	Allday
HUNTER	P284	1983	Allday
STRIKER	P285	1984	Allday

Displacement 34 tons **Dimensions** 20m x 5m x 1m **Speed** 24 knots **Complement** 11.

Notes
Seamanship & Navigational training vessels for the Royal Naval Reserve & University RN Units. Based on a successful design used by HM Customs. Ships are based at Glasgow, Aberdeen, Southampton, London and Liverpool respectively.

HMS Messina

MANLY CLASS

Ship	Pennant Number	Completion Date	Builder
MANLY	A92	1982	R. Dunston
MENTOR	A94	1982	R. Dunston
MILBROOK	A97	1982	R. Dunston
MESSINA	A107	1982	R. Dunston

Displacement 127 tons **Dimensions** 25m x 6m x 2m **Speed** 10 knots **Complement** 9/13.

Notes
Very similar to the RMAS/RNXS tenders. These four craft are all employed on training duties (first three named attached to HMS RALEIGH for new entry training). MESSINA is a training ship for Royal Marines based at Poole. IXWORTH (A318), ETTRICK (A274), ELSING (A277), IRONBRIDGE (A311) & DATCHET (A357) are all former RMAS tenders now flying the White Ensign.

HMS Roebuck

ROEBUCK CLASS

Ship	Pennant Number	Completion Date	Builder
ROEBUCK	A130	1986	Brooke Marine

Displacement 1500 tonnes **Dimensions** 64m x 13m x 4m **Speed** 15 knots **Complement** 47.

Notes
Was due to replace HECLA in the Survey fleet until the latter reprieved in 1987 for further service. Fitted with the latest fixing aids and sector scanning sonar.

43

SURVEY SHIPS

HMS Herald

HECLA CLASS

Ship	Pennant Number	Completion Date	Builder
HECLA	A133	1965	Yarrow
HECATE	A137	1965	Yarrow
HERALD	A138	1974	Robb Caledon

Displacement 2,733 tons **Dimensions** 79m x 15m x 5m **Speed** 14 knots **Complement** 115.

Notes
Able to operate for long periods away from shore support, these ships and the smaller ships of the Hydrographic Fleet collect the data that is required to produce the Admiralty Charts and publications which are sold to mariners worldwide. HERALD is an improved version of the earlier ships. Plans to dispose of HECLA and HECATE in 1987/8 were abandoned. HECATE now expected to be sold late 1990 or 1991.

BULLDOG CLASS

HMS Beagle

Ship	Pennant Number	Completion Date	Builder
BULLDOG	A317	1968	Brooke Marine
BEAGLE	A319	1968	Brooke Marine
FAWN	A335	1968	Brooke Marine

Displacement 1,088 tons **Dimensions** 60m x 11m x 4m **Speed** 15 knots **Complement** 39.

Notes
Designed to operate in coastal waters. All due to be extensively refitted to extend hull life into the 1990's. FOX sold for commercial service in December 1988.
GLEANER (A86) is a small inshore survey craft based at Portsmouth.

45

HMS Challenger

SEABED OPERATIONS VESSEL

Ship	Pennant Number	Completion Date	Builder
CHALLENGER	K07	1984	Scott Lithgow

Displacement 6,400 tons **Dimensions** 134m x 18m x 5m **Speed** 15 knots **Complement** 185.

Notes

CHALLENGER is equipped to find, inspect and, where appropriate, recover objects from the seabed at greater depths than is currently possible. She is designed with a saturation diving system enabling up to 12 men to live in comfort for long periods in a decompression chamber amidships, taking their turns to be lowered in a diving bell to work on the seabed. Also fitted to carry out salvage work. Now operational after a series of delays during building and acceptance trials.

● HMY BRITANNIA

HMY Britannia

ROYAL YACHT

Ship	Pennant Number	Completion Date	Builder
BRITANNIA	A00	1954	J. Brown

Displacement 5,280 tons **Dimensions** 126m x 17m x 5m **Speed** 21 knots **Complement** 250.

Notes
Probably the best known ship in the Royal Navy, BRITANNIA was designed to be converted to a hospital ship in time of war but this conversion was not made during the Falklands crisis. Is available for use in NATO exercises when not on 'Royal' business. Normally to be seen in Portsmouth Harbour when not away on official duties. The only seagoing ship in the RN commanded by an Admiral.

47

HMS Endurance

ICE PATROL SHIP

Ship	Pennant Number	Completion Date	Builder
ENDURANCE (ex MV Anita Dan)	A171	1956	Krogerwerft Rendsburg

Displacement 3,600 tons **Dimensions** 93m x 14m x 5m **Speed** 14 knots **Armament** 2 x 20mm guns **Aircraft** 2 Lynx **Complement** 124.

Notes
Purchased from Denmark in 1967. ENDURANCE is painted brilliant red for easy identification in the ice of Antarctica where she spends 6 months of the year. Her role is to undertake oceanographic and hydrographic surveys in the area and support scientists working ashore. A small Royal Marine detachment is embarked. Was to have been "retired early" after her 1982 season in Antarctica, but reprieved as a result of the Falklands crisis.

HMS Ark Royal

HMS York

HMS Active

HMS Brecon

M29

HMS Penelope

HMS Sandpiper

HM Ships Invincible (top), Illustrious and Ark Royal

HMS Nottingham

THE NAVY'S MISSILES

SEA SKUA

An anti-surface ship missile. It is carried by the Lynx helicopter.

SEACAT

A close-range anti-aircraft missile. Control is by radar tracking and visual guidance. Propulsion is by solid fuel. It is fitted in older frigates.

SEA DART

A ship-to-air medium-range missile with anti-ship capability. Propulsion is by ramjet and solid boost. It is carried in aircraft carriers and destroyers.

SEA WOLF

A high speed close-range anti-missile and anti-aircraft missile with fully automatic radar control and guidance. It is fitted in some frigates.

EXOCET

A medium-range surface-to-surface missile with a very low trajectory and a radar homing head. It is carried in some frigates.

SIDEWINDER

An infra-red homing air-to-air missile. It has a solid propellant motor and a high explosive warhead. It is carried on the Sea Harrier.

SEA EAGLE

A long-range autonomous sea-skimming anti-ship missile. It is carried on the Sea Harrier.

SUB HARPOON

A long-range anti-ship missile launched from a submerged submarine. It is the principal anti-surface ship armament of the Fleet submarines. Harpoon is the "above water version" for later Type 22 and Type 23 frigates.

STING-RAY

The most sophisticated homing torpedo in service. It can be fired from deck-mounted tubes or dropped by helicopter.

POLARIS

Submarine-launched ballistic missile fitted with nuclear warheads. It has a range of 2,500 nautical miles with solid-fuel propulsion.

THE ROYAL FLEET AUXILIARY

The Royal Fleet Auxiliary Service (RFA) is a civilian manned fleet owned and operated by the Ministry of Defence. Its main task is to supply warships of the Royal Navy at sea with fuel, food, stores and ammunition which they need to remain operational while away from base. With so few bases overseas which can be guaranteed in time of tension—let alone during any conflict it has become vital, over the years, that everything from the smallest nut and bolt to a complete aero engine is taken on any naval deployment away from our coasts. The lack of that nut and bolt could well stop a ship in its tracks—literally. Increasingly, the service also provides aviation support for the Royal Navy—together with amphibious support and secure sea transport for army units and their equipment.

During recent years the reduction of the size of this vital "navy within a navy" must be viewed with concern. Last year (1989) three ships were deleted from the fleet and two others laid up as economy measures.

These moves obviously reflect the shrinking size of the fleet they support but days doubtless lie ahead when deployments away from these shores—beit for operations or exercises will have to be curtailed for lack of fleet support. In the longer term with no new ships on the order books it looks as if naval deployments will have to be grouped around one huge RFA. How single ship deployments to the West Indies, Gulf, Iceland/UK gap are to be supported remains a mystery. The new "one stop" AOR ships are not going to have much time to stop themselves (for re-fit/repairs) unless new smaller ships are designed and ordered soon.

The men of the RFA service have long boasted they are "ready for anything"—but with a decreasing number of (aging) hulls they may well have to choose their words more carefully in the days that lie ahead.

SHIPS OF THE ROYAL FLEET AUXILIARY
Pennant Numbers

Ship	Penn No.	Ship	Penn No.	Ship	Penn. No.
TIDESPRING	A75	DILIGENCE	A132	FORT AUSTIN	A386
BRAMBLELEAF	A81	ARGUS	A135	RESOURCE	A480
BAYLEAF	A109	GREEN ROVER	A268	REGENT	A486
ORANGELEAF	A110	GREY ROVER	A269	SIR BEDIVERE	L3004
OAKLEAF	A111	BLUE ROVER	A270	SIR GALAHAD	L3005
OLWEN	A122	GOLD ROVER	A271	SIR GERAINT	L3027
OLNA	A123	BLACK ROVER	A273	SIR PERCIVALE	L3036
OLMEDA	A124	FORT GRANGE	A385	SIR TRISTRAM	L3505

RFA Olmeda

'OL' CLASS

Ship	Pennant Number	Completion Date	Builder
OLWEN	A122	1965	Hawthorn Leslie
OLNA	A123	1966	Hawthorn Leslie
OLMEDA	A124	1965	Swan Hunter

Displacement 36,000 tons **Dimensions** 197m x 26m x 10m **Speed** 19 knots **Complement** 92.

Notes

These ships can operate up to 3 Sea King helicopters. Dry stores can be carried—and transferred at sea—as well as a wide range of fuel, aviation spirit and lubricants. Now somewhat 'over age', considerable sums are being spent to give these ships extra life.

**T
A
N
K
E
R
S**

RFA Tidespring

TIDE CLASS

Ship	Pennant Number	Completion Date	Builder
TIDESPRING	A75	1963	Hawthorn Leslie

Displacement 27,400 tons **Dimensions** 177m x 22m x 10m **Speed** 18 knots **Complement** 98.

Notes
Built to fuel warships at sea in any part of the world. Strengthened for ice operations. A hangar and flight deck provides space for two Sea King helicopters if required. Was due to be "retired early" during 1982/3 but reprieved for Falklands crisis and remains in service despite her age. Expected to be retired in mid 1990.

RFA Green Rover

ROVER CLASS

Ship	Pennant Number	Completion Date	Builder
GREEN ROVER ● A268		1969	Swan Hunter
GREY ROVER	A269	1970	Swan Hunter
BLUE ROVER	A270	1970	Swan Hunter
GOLD ROVER	A271	1974	Swan Hunter
BLACK ROVER	A273	1974	Swan Hunter

Displacement 11,522 tons **Dimensions** 141m x 19m x 7m **Speed** 18 knots **Complement** 49-54.

Notes
Small Fleet Tankers designed to supply HM ships with fresh water, dry cargo and refrigerated provisions as well as a range of fuel and lubricants. Helicopter deck but no hangar. ● In reserve.

RFA Oakleaf

LEAF CLASS

Ship	Pennant Number	Completion Date	Builder
BRAMBLELEAF	A81	1980	Cammell Laird
BAYLEAF	A109	1982	Cammell Laird
ORANGELEAF	A110	1982	Cammell Laird
OAKLEAF	A111	1981	Uddevalla

Displacement 37,747 tons **Dimensions** 170m x 26m x 12m **Speed** 14.5 knots **Complement** 60.

Notes
All are ex merchant ships. BRAMBLELEAF is owned by MOD (N), the remainder are on bare boat charter. OAKLEAF (ex OKTANIA) differs from the other ships of the class which are all commercial Stat 32 tankers. At 49,310 tons she is the largest vessel in RFA/RN service. APPLELEAF taken over by Royal Australian Navy (as HMAS Westralia) in late 1989.

RFA Fort Grange

FORT CLASS

Ship	Pennant Number	Completion Date	Builder
FORT GRANGE	A385	1978	Scott Lithgow
FORT AUSTIN	A386	1979	Scott Lithgow

Displacement 23,384 tons **Dimensions** 183m x 24m x 9m **Speed** 20 knots **Complement** 201, (120 RFA, 36 RNSTS & 45 RN).

Notes
Full hangar and maintenance facilities are provided and up to four Sea King helicopters can be carried for both the transfer of stores and anti-submarine protection of a group of ships. Both ships can be armed with 4 x 20mm guns mounted on the Scot platforms. Both are fitted with 3″ Chaff Systems.
Two ships, of a new class of "one stop" ships, to be named FORT VICTORIA and FORT GEORGE, are under construction.

S
T
O
R
E

S
H
I
P
S

RFA Regent

REGENT CLASS

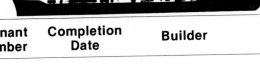

Ship	Pennant Number	Completion Date	Builder
RESOURCE	A480	1967	Scotts
REGENT	A486	1967	Harland & Wolff

Displacement 22,890 **Dimensions** 195m x 24m x 8m **Speed** 21 knots **Complement** 182, (RFA 112, RNSTS 37, RN 11).

Notes
The widest range of naval armament stores are carried onboard plus a limited range of general naval stores and food. When the Wessex 5 was withdrawn from service in April 1987 both ships lost their permanently embarked helicopter but they retain full flight deck facilities. REGENT in Preservation by operation (Reserve) at Rosyth in late 1989.

RFA Sir Galahad

LANDING SHIPS
SIR LANCELOT CLASS

Ship	Pennant Number	Completion Date	Builder
SIR BEDIVERE	L3004	1967	Hawthorn
SIR GERAINT	L3027	1967	Stephen
SIR PERCIVALE	L3036	1968	Hawthorn
SIR TRISTRAM	L3505	1967	Hawthorn
SIR GALAHAD	L3005	1987	Swan Hunter

Displacement 5,550 tons **Dimensions** 126m x 18m x 4m **Speed** 17 knots **Armament** Can be fitted with 2 x 40mm guns in emergency **Complement** 65, SIR GALAHAD (8,451 tons. 140m x 20m Complement 58.)

Notes
Manned by the RFA but tasked by the Army, these ships are used for heavy secure transport of stores—embarked by bow and stern doors —and beach assault landings. Can operate helicopters from tank deck if required. SIR LANCELOT sold for commercial service in 1989.

● OFFICIAL PHOTO

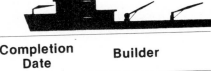

RFA Diligence

Ship	Pennant Number	Completion Date	Builder
DILIGENCE	A132	1981	Oresundsvarvet

Displacement 5,814 tons **Dimensions** 120m x 12m **Speed** 15 knots **Armament** 2 x 20mm **Complement** RFA 40. RN Personnel — approx 100.

Notes
Formerly the M/V Stena Inspector purchased (£25m) for service in the South Atlantic. Accommodation is provided for a 100 man Fleet Maintenance Unit. Her deep diving complex was removed and workshops added. Has given valuable support to a wide range of warships in the Falklands and Gulf.

● OFFICIAL PHOTO

RFA Argus

Ship	Pennant Number	Completion Date	Builder
ARGUS	A135	1981	Cantieri Navali Breda

Displacement 28,081 tons (full load) **Dimensions** 175m x 30m x 8m **Speed** 18 knots **Armament** 4 x 30mm. 2 x 20mm **Complement** 254 (inc 137 Air Group) **Aircraft** 6 Sea King, 12 Harriers can be carried in a "ferry role".

Notes
Formerly the M/V CONTENDER BEZANT taken up from trade during the Falklands crisis. Purchased in 1984 (£13 million) for conversion to an 'Aviation Training Ship'. A £50 million re-build was undertaken at Belfast from 1984-87. Replaced ENGADINE during 1989. Based at Portland.

67

ROYAL MARITIME
AUXILIARY SERVICE

The Royal Maritime Auxiliary Service Fleet is comprised of over 500 hulls, of which 310 are self propelled, including small harbour launches, the remainder being dumb craft such as lighters etc. It is administered by the Director of Marine Services (Naval) to whom the Captains of the Ports and Resident Naval Officers at the various Naval Bases are mainly responsible for the provision of Marine Services to the Royal Navy. The RMAS also provides many types of craft for the numerous and diverse requirements of other Ministry of Defence departments.

Ships of the RMAS, which can be seen at work in all the Naval Bases throughout the United Kingdom and at Gibraltar, are easily identified by their black hulls, buff coloured superstructure and funnels, and by the RMAS flag, which is a blue ensign defaced in the fly by a yellow anchor over two wavy lines. Pennant numbers are painted only on those vessels that are normally employed outside harbour limits.

SHIPS OF THE ROYAL MARITIME AUXILIARY SERVICE — PENNANT NUMBERS

Ship	Penn. No.	Ship	Penn. No.
MELTON	A83	EXPRESS	A167
MENAI	A84	LABRADOR	A168
MEON	A87	KITTY	A170
MILFORD	A91	LESLEY	A172
BEMBRIDGE	A101	DOROTHY	A173
ALSATIAN	A106	LILAH	A174
FELICITY	A112	MARY	A175
MAGNET	A114	EDITH	A177
LODESTONE	A115	HUSKY	A178
CAIRN	A126	MASTIFF	A180
TORRENT	A127	IRENE	A181
TORRID	A128	SALUKI	A182
DALMATION	A129	ISABEL	A183
TORNADO	A140	SALMOOR	A185
TORCH	A141	SALMASTER	A186
TORMENTOR	A142	SALMAID	A187
TOREADOR	A143	POINTER	A188
WATERMAN	A146	SETTER	A189
FRANCES	A147	JOAN	A190
FIONA	A148	JOYCE	A193
FLORENCE	A149	GWENDOLINE	A196
GENEVIEVE	A150	SEALYHAM	A197
GEORGINA	A152	HELEN	A198
EXAMPLE	A153	MYRTLE	A199
EXPLORER	A154	SPANIEL	A201
DEERHOUND	A155	NANCY	A202
DAPHNE	A156	NORAH	A205
LOYAL HELPER	A157	LLANDOVERY	A207
SUPPORTER	A158	LAMLASH	A208
LOYAL WATCHER	A159	LECHLADE	A211
LOYAL VOLUNTEER	A160	ENDEAVOUR	A213
LOYAL MEDIATOR	A161	BEE	A216
ELKHOUND	A162	LOYAL	
EXPLOIT	A163	MODERATOR	A220
GOOSANDER	A164	FORCEFUL	A221
POCHARD	A165	NIMBLE	A222
KATHLEEN	A166	POWERFUL	A223

Ship	Penn. No.	Ship	Penn. No.
ADEPT	A224	GLENCOE	A392
BUSTLER	A225	DUNSTER	A393
CAPABLE	A226	FINTRY	A394
CAREFUL	A227	GRASMERE	A402
FAITHFUL	A228	CROMARTY	A488
CRICKET	A229	DORNOCH	A490
COCKCHAFER	A230	ROLLICKER	A502
DEXTEROUS	A231	HEADCORN	A1766
GNAT	A239	HEVER	A1767
SHEEPDOG	A250	HARLECH	A1768
LYDFORD	A251	HAMBLEDON	A1769
LADYBIRD	A253	LOYAL	
MEAVEY	A254	CHANCELLOR	A1770
CICALA	A263	LOYAL PROCTOR	A1771
SCARAB	A272	HOLMWOOD	A1772
AURICULA	A285	HORNING	A1773
ILCHESTER	A308	MANDARIN	P192
INSTOW	A309	GARGANEY	P194
FOXHOUND	A326	GOLDENEYE	P195
BASSET	A327	ALNMOUTH	Y13
COLLIE	A328	WATERSHED	Y18
CORGI	A330	WATERSPOUT	Y19
FOTHERBY	A341	WATERSIDE	Y20
FELSTEAD	A348	OILPRESS	Y21
ELKSTONE	A353	OILSTONE	Y22
FROXFIELD	A354	OILWELL	Y23
EPWORTH	A355	OILFIELD	Y24
ROYSTERER	A361	OILBIRD	Y25
DENMEAD	A363	OILMAN	Y26
WHITEHEAD	A364	WATERCOURSE	Y30
FULBECK	A365	WATERFOWL	Y31
ROBUST	A366	MOORHEN	Y32
NEWTON	A367	MOORFOWL	Y33
WARDEN	A368		
KINTERBURY	A378		
THROSK	A379		
CRICKLADE	A381		
ARROCHAR	A382		
CLOVELLY	A389		
CRICCIETH	A391		

RMAS Robust

ROYSTERER CLASS

Ship	Pennant Number	Completion Date	Builder
ROYSTERER	A361	1972	C.D. Holmes
ROBUST	A366	1974	C.D. Holmes
ROLLICKER	A502	1973	C.D. Holmes

G.R.T. 1,036 tons **Dimensions** 54m x 12m x 6m **Speed** 15 knots **Complement** 21.

Notes
Built for salvage and long range towage, a role they only fulfil infrequently. They are, however used for various "deepwater" trials for MOD research departments.

T
U
G
S

71

W. SARTORI

RMAS Powerful

HARBOUR TUGS
TWIN UNIT TRACTOR TUGS (TUTT'S)

Ship	Pennant Number	Completion Date	Builder
FORCEFUL	A221	1985	R. Dunston
NIMBLE	A222	1985	R. Dunston
POWERFUL	A223	1985	R. Dunston
ADEPT	A224	1980	R. Dunston
BUSTLER	A225	1981	R. Dunston
CAPABLE	A226	1981	R. Dunston
CAREFUL	A227	1982	R. Dunston
FAITHFUL	A228	1985	R. Dunston
DEXTEROUS	A231	1986	R. Dunston

G.R.T. 375 tons **Dimensions** 39m x 10m x 4m **Speed** 12 knots
Complement 9

Notes
The principle harbour tug in naval service. CAPABLE is at
Gibraltar.

G. DAVIES

RMAS Foxhound

DOG CLASS

Ship	Penn. No.	Ship	Penn. No.
ALSATIAN	A106	POINTER	A188
CAIRN ●	A126	SETTER	A189
DALMATIAN	A129	SEALYHAM	A197
DEERHOUND	A155	SPANIEL	A201
ELKHOUND	A162	SHEEPDOG	A250
LABRADOR	A168	FOXHOUND	A326
HUSKY	A178	BASSET	A327
MASTIFF	A180	COLLIE ●	A328
SALUKI	A182	CORGI	A330

G.R.T. 152 tons **Dimensions** 29m x 8m x 4m **Speed** 12 knots
Complement 5

Notes
General harbour tugs — all completed between 1962 & 1972.
● No longer tugs. Refitted as trials vessels for service at Kyle of Lochalsh.
   The long term replacement of these vessels is now a priority.
Two Triton tugs have been ordered as possible replacements.

RMAS Dorothy

IMPROVED GIRL CLASS

Ship	Penn. No.	Ship	Penn. No.
DAPHNE	A156	EDITH	A177
DOROTHY	A173		

G.R.T. 75 tons **Speed** 10 knots **Complement** 4

Notes
All completed 1971-2. DAISY, DORIS, CHARLOTTE and CHRISTINE sold 1989.

W. SARTORI

RMAS Norah

IRENE CLASS

Ship	Penn. No.	Ship	Penn. No.
KATHLEEN	A166	ISABEL	A183
KITTY	A170	JOAN	A190
LESLEY	A172	JOYCE	A193
LILAH	A174	MYRTLE	A199
MARY	A175	NANCY	A202
IRENE	A181	NORAH	A205

G.R.T. 89 tons **Speed** 8 knots **Complement** 4

Notes
Known as Water Tractors these craft are used for basin moves and towage of light barges.

75

G. DAVIES

RMAS Fiona

FELICITY CLASS

Ship	Penn. No.	Ship	Penn. No.
FELICITY	A112	GENEVIEVE	A150
FRANCES	A147	GEORGINA	A152
FIONA	A148	GWENDOLINE	A196
FLORENCE	A149	HELEN	A198

G.R.T. 80 tons **Speed** 10 knots **Complement** 4

Notes
Water Tractors — completed in 1973; FRANCES, FLORENCE & GENEVIEVE completed 1980.

M. LENNON

RMAS Newton

Ship	Pennant Number	Completion Date	Builder
NEWTON	A367	1976	Scotts

G.R.T. 2,779 tons **Dimensions** 99m x 16m x 6m **Speed** 15 knots **Complement** 39

Notes
Built as sonar propagation trials ship but can also be used as a Cable Layer.
The Trials ship WHITEHEAD (A364) laid up (at Devonport) in long term reserve. A mid life refit cancelled as no new role found for the ship.

M. LENNON

RMAS Auricula

TEST & EXPERIMENTAL SONAR TENDER

Ship	Pennant Number	Completion Date	Builder
AURICULA	A285	1981	Ferguson Bros

G.R.T. 981 tons **Dimensions** 52m x 11m x 3m **Speed** 12 knots
Complement 20

Notes
Employed on evaluation work of new sonar equipment that may
equip RN ships of the future. Based at Portland.

W. SARTORI

RMAS Arrochar

ARMAMENT STORES CARRIERS

Ship	Pennant Number	Completion Date	Builder
KINTERBURY	A378	1980	Appledore SB
THROSK	A379	1977	Cleland SB Co.
ARROCHAR	A382	1981	Appledore SB

G.R.T. 1,357 tons **Dimensions** 64m x 12m x 5m **Speed** 14 knots **Complement** 19

Notes
2 holds carry Naval armament stores, ammunition and guided missiles. All three vessels vary slightly. ARROCHAR (ex ST GEORGE) taken over in late 1988 from the Army. Only KINTERBURY operational, others in reserve at Portsmouth. THROSK is surplus to requirements and a new role may be found for her.

M. LENNON

RMAS Scarab

INSECT CLASS

Ship	Pennant Number	Completion Date	Builder
BEE	A216	1970	C.D. Holmes
CRICKET	A229	1972	Beverley
COCKCHAFER	A230	1971	Beverley
GNAT	A239	1972	Beverley
LADYBIRD	A253	1973	Beverley
CICALA	A263	1971	Beverley
SCARAB	A272	1973	Beverley

G.R.T. 279 tons **Dimensions** 34m x 8m x 3m **Speed** 10.5 knots **Complement** 7-9

Notes
CRICKET and SCARAB are fitted as Mooring Vessels and COCKCHAFER as a Trials Stores Carrier — remainder are Naval Armament carriers.

80

RNXS Loyal Mediator

LOYAL CLASS

Ship	Penn. No.	Ship	Penn. No.
LOYAL HELPER	A157	LOYAL MEDIATOR	A161
SUPPORTER	A158	LOYAL MODERATOR	A220
LOYAL WATCHER	A159	LOYAL CHANCELLOR	A1770
LOYAL VOLUNTEER	A160	LOYAL PROCTOR	A1771

G.R.T. 112 tons **Dimensions** 24m x 6m x 3m **Speed** 10.5 knots **Complement** 24

Notes

All these craft are operated by the Royal Naval Auxiliary Service (RNXS)—men (and women)—who in time of emergency would man these craft for duties as port control vessels.

T
E
N
D
E
R
S

M. LOUAGIE

RMAS Horning

(TYPE A, B & X) TENDERS

Ship	Penn. No.	Ship	Penn. No.
MELTON	A83	FULBECK	A365
MENAI	A84	CRICKLADE	A381
MEON	A87	CLOVELLY	A389
MILFORD	A91	CRICCIETH	A391
LLANDOVERY	A207	GLENCOE	A392
LAMLASH	A208	DUNSTER	A393
LECHLADE	A211	FINTRY	A394
LYDFORD	A251	GRASMERE	A402
MEAVEY	A254	CROMARTY	A488
ILCHESTER*	A308	DORNOCH	A490
INSTOW*	A309	HEADCORN	A1766
FOTHERBY	A341	HEVER	A1767
FELSTEAD	A348	HARLECH	A1768
ELKSTONE	A353	HAMBLEDON	A1769
FROXFIELD	A354	HOLMWOOD	A1772
EPWORTH	A355	HORNING	A1773
DENMEAD	A363	DATCHET	A357

G.R.T. 78 tons **Dimensions** 24m x 6m x 3m **Speed** 10.5 knots
Complement 4/5

Notes
All completed since 1971 to replace Motor Fishing Vessels.
Vessels marked* are diving tenders. Remainder are Training
Tenders, Passenger Ferries, or Cargo Vessels. GLENCOE and
DENMEAD on loan to the RNXS—and painted grey.

M WILLIS

RMAS Bembridge

ABERDOVEY CLASS ('63 DESIGN)

Ship	Penn. No.	Ship	Penn. No.
ALNMOUTH	Y13	BEMBRIDGE	A101

G.R.T. 77 tons **Dimensions** 24m x 5m x 3m **Speed** 10.5 knots **Complement** 4/5

Notes
ALNMOUTH is a Sea Cadet Training Ship based at Plymouth, BEMBRIDGE has a similar role at Portsmouth. Other vessels of the class now used by Sea Cadet/RNR Units.

XSV Explorer

COASTAL TRAINING CRAFT
EXAMPLE CLASS

Ship	Pennant Number	Completion Date	Builder
XSV EXAMPLE	A153	1985	Watercraft
XSV EXPLORER	A154	1985	Watercraft
XSV EXPLOIT	A163	1988	Vosper T
XSV EXPRESS	A167	1988	Vosper T

Displacement 43 tons **Dimensions** 20m x 6m x 1m **Speed** 20 knots
Armament Nil **Complement** 14

Notes
Training vessels for the RNXS. In wartime would be used within
ports/anchorages on port control duties.

B. McCALL

OILPRESS CLASS

Ship	Pennant Number	Completion Date	Builder
OILPRESS	Y21	1969	Appledore Shipbuilders
OILSTONE	Y22	1969	" "
OILWELL	Y23	1969	" "
OILFIELD	Y24	1969	" "
OILBIRD	Y25	1969	" "
OILMAN	Y26	1969	" "

G.R.T. 362 tons **Dimensions** 41m x 9m x 3m **Speed** 11 knots **Complement** 5

Notes
Employed as Harbour and Coastal Oilers. OILFIELD is in reserve at Portsmouth.

W. SARTORI

WATER CARRIERS
WATER CLASS

Ship	Pennant Number	Completion Date	Builder
WATERSHED	Y18	1967	Drypool Eng Co
WATERSPOUT	Y19	1967	Drypool Eng Co
WATERSIDE	Y20	1968	Drypool Eng Co
WATERCOURSE	Y30	1974	Drypool Eng Co
WATERFOWL	Y31	1974	Drypool Eng Co
WATERMAN	A146	1978	R. Dunston

G.R.T. 263 tons **Dimensions** 40m x 8m x 2m **Speed** 11 knots
Complement 5

Notes
Capable of coastal passages, these craft normally supply either demineralised or fresh water to the Fleet within port limits.
The hulk of the former WATERFALL is used as a diver training facility.

86

M. LENNON

RMAS Magnet

DEGAUSSING VESSELS
MAGNET CLASS

Ship	Pennant Number	Completion Date	Builder
MAGNET	A114	1979	Cleland
LODESTONE	A115	1980	Cleland

G.R.T. 828 tons **Dimensions** 55m x 12m x 4m **Speed** 14 knots
Complement 9

Notes
One ship is normally operational, the other kept in reserve.

M. LENNON

RMAS Torrid

TORPEDO RECOVERY VESSELS (TRV'S)
TORRID CLASS

Ship	Pennant Number	Completion Date	Builder
TORRENT	A127	1971	Cleland SB Co
TORRID	A128	1972	Cleland SB Co

G.R.T. 550 tons **Dimensions** 46m x 9m x 3m **Speed** 12 knots
Complement 14

Notes
A stern ramp is built for the recovery of torpedoes fired for trials
and exercises. A total of 32 can be carried.
TORRID placed in reserve in 1989 as an economy measure.

RMAS Tornado

TORNADO CLASS

Ship	Pennant Number	Completion Date	Builder
TORNADO	A140	1979	Hall Russell
TORCH	A141	1980	Hall Russell
TORMENTOR	A142	1980	Hall Russell
TOREADOR	A143	1980	Hall Russell

G.R.T. 560 tons **Dimensions** 47m x 8m x 3m **Speed** 14 knots **Complement** 13

Notes
TORCH is based at Portland, TORMENTOR at Plymouth — remainder on the Clyde.

T
R
V
's

W. SARTORI

RMAS Salmoor

SAL CLASS

Ship	Pennant Number	Completion Date	Builder
SALMOOR	A185	1985	Hall Russell
SALMASTER	A186	1986	Hall Russell
SALMAID	A187	1986	Hall Russell

Displacement 2200 tonnes **Dimensions** 77m x 15m x 4m **Speed** 15 knots **Complement** 17

Notes
Built at a cost of £9 million each these ships have replaced the 40-year-old Kin class. They are multi-purpose vessels designed to lay and maintain underwater targets and moorings and undertake a wide range of salvage tasks.

W. SARTORI

RMAS Mandarin

WILD DUCK CLASS

Ship	Pennant Number	Completion Date	Builder
MANDARIN	P192	1964	C. Laird
GARGANEY	P194	1966	Brooke Marine
GOLDENEYE	P195	1966	Brooke Marine
GOOSANDER	A164	1973	Robb Caledon
POCHARD	A165	1973	Robb Caledon

G.R.T. 900 tons* **Dimensions** 58mm x 12m x 4m **Speed** 10 knots
Complement 18
* Vessels vary slightly

Notes
Vessels capable of carrying out a wide range of duties laying moorings and heavy lift salvage work. 200 tons can be lifted over over the bow.

91

M
S
V
's

A. ELLIS

RMAS Moorhen

MOOR CLASS

Ship	Pennant Number	Completion Date	Builder
MOORHEN	Y32	1989	McTay Marine
MOORFOWL	Y33	1989	McTay Marine

Displacement 518 tons **Dimensions** 32m x 11m x 2m **Speed** 8 knots **Complement** 10

Notes
Powered mooring lighters for use within harbour limits.

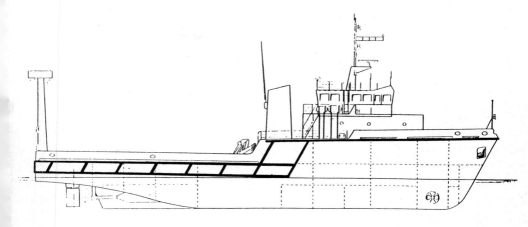

RMAS Warden

WARDEN CLASS

Ship	Pennant Number	Completion Date	Builder
WARDEN	A368	1989	Richards

Displacement 626 tons **Dimensions** 48m x 10m x4m **Speed** 15 knots **Complement**

Notes
Due for completion in early 1990 to replace DOLWEN as the Range Mooring Vessel for RAE Aberporth (S. Wales). Based at Pembroke Dock.

HMAV Ardennes

ARMY LANDING CRAFT

LCL CLASS

LANDING CRAFT LOGISTIC

Vessel	Pennant Number	Completion Date	Builder
HMAV Ardennes	L4001	1977	Brooke Marine
HMAV Arakan	L4003	1978	Brooke Marine

Displacement 1,050 tons **Dimensions** 72m x 15m x 2m **Speed** 10 knots **Complement** 36

Notes

Designed to carry up to 520 tonnes of cargo, overside loaded, or up to Five Chieftain tanks—Ro Ro laoded, reducing to 254 tonnes for beaching opreations, through bow doors. Principal roles are maintenance of the Royal Artillery Range Outer Hebrides and in support of Amphibious Operations and Exercises.

M. LOUAGIE

RCTV Andalsnes

RCL CLASS   RAMPED CRAFT LOGISTIC

Vessel	Pennant Number	Completion Date	Builder
RCTV Arromanches	L105	1981	Brooke Marine
RCTV Antwerp	L106	1981	Brooke Marine
RCTV Andalsnes	L107	1984	James & Stone
RCTV Abbeville	L108	1985	James & Stone
RCTV Akyab	L109	1985	James & Stone
RCTV Aachen	L110	1986	McTay Marine
RCTV Arezzo	L111	1986	McTay Marine
RCTV Agheila	L112	1987	McTay Marine
RCTV Audemer	L113	1987	McTay Marine

Displacement 165 tons **Dimensions** 30m x 8m x 2m **Speed** 9 knots
Complement 6

Notes
Smaller—"all purpose" landing craft capable of carrying up to
100 tons. In service in coastal waters around Cyprus, Hong Kong
& UK.

**AIRCRAFT
OF THE FLEET AIR ARM**

British Aerospace Sea Harrier

Variants: FRS 1 (FRS 2 undergoing development).
Role: Short take off, vertical landing (STOVL) fighter, reconnaissence and strike aircraft.
Engine: 1 x 21,500lb thrust Rolls Royce PEGASUS 104, 106 turbojet.
Span 25'3" **length** 47'7" **height** 12'0" **max weight** 26,200lb.
Max speed Mach 1.2 **Crew** 1 pilot.
Avionics: Blue Fox pulse radar. (To be replaced by the Blue Vixen pulse doppler radar in the FRS 2).
Armament: SEA EAGLE air to surface missiles. SIDEWINDER air to air missiles. (FRS 2 to carry the new Anglo/US AMRAAM radar guided air to air missiles). 2 x 30mm Aden cannons with 120 rounds per gun in detachable pods, one either side of the lower fuselage. 1 fuselage centreline and 4 underwing hardpoints. The inner wing stations are capable of carrying 2,000lb of stores and are plumbed for drop tanks. The other positions can carry stores up to 1,000lb in weight. Possible loads include 1,000lb, 500lb or practice bombs; BL 755 cluster bombs, Lepus flares, 190 or 100 gallon drop tanks. A single F95 camera is mounted obliquely in the nose for the reconnaissence role. The prototype FRS 2 first flew in September 1988.
Squadron Service: 800, 801 and 899 squadrons in commission.
Notes: During 1990, 800 squadron will be embarked in HMS INVINCIBLE and 801 in HMS ARK ROYAL. 899 squadron is responsible for the training of replacement pilots and the development of tactics and is normally shore based at RNAS YEOVILTON. In a period of tension it could embark to reinforce the embarked air groups in the carriers.

97

Westland SEA KING

Developed for the Royal Navy from the Sikorsky SH3D, the basic Seaking airframe is used in three different roles. The following details are common to all:
Engines 2 x 1600shp Rolls Royce Gnome H 1400—1 free power turbines.
Rotor Diameter 62′ 0″ **Length** 54′9″ **Height** 17′2″**Max Weight** 23,500lb **Max Speed** 120 knots.
The 3 versions àre:-

HAS 5

Roles: Anti-submarine search and strike. SAR. Transport.
Crew: 2 pilots, 1 observer and 1 aircrewman.
Avionics: MEL Sea Searcher radar; Plessey Type 195 variable depth active/passive sonar. GEC LAPADS passive sonobuoy analyses. Marconi Orange Crop passive ESM equipment.
Armament: 4 fuselage hardpoints capable of carrying STINGRAY, Mk 46/Mk 44 torpedoes or depth charges. Various flares, markers, grenades and sonobuoys can be carried internally and hand launched. A 7.62mm machine gun can be mounted in the doorway.
Squadron Service: 706, 810, 814, 819, 820 and 826 squadrons in commission.
Notes: The Seaking has been the backbone of the Fleet Air Arm's anti-submarine force since 1970. A further improved version, the HAS 6 is entering service. 706 is the advanced training squadron at RNAS CULDROSE. 810 is an operational training squadron with the capability to embark to reinforce the front line. During 1990, 814 squadron will be embarked in HMS INVINCIBLE and 820 in HMS ARK ROYAL. 819 is shore based at PRESTWICK and 826 provides flights for service in frigates and RFA ships. The HAS 5 has a noteable SAR capability which is frequently demonstrated in the south west approaches.

AEW 2

Role: Airborne Early Warning. **Crew**: 1 pilot and 2 observers.
Avionics: Thorn/EMI searchwater radar. Marconi Orange Crop passive ESM equipment.
Armament: Nil.
Squadron Service: 849 HQ, 849A and 849B flights in commission.
Notes: Used to detect low flying aircraft trying to attack aircraft carrier battle groups under shipborne radar cover. Can also be used for surface search utilising its sophisticated, computerised long range radar. During 1990 849A flight will be embarked in HMS INVINCIBLE and 849B in HMS ARK ROYAL. 849HQ acts as a training and trials unit at RNAS CULDROSE.

HC 4

Role: Commando assault and utility transport.
Avionics: —
Crew: 1 pilot and 1 aircrewman.
Armament: Door mounted 7.62mm machine gun.
Squadron Service: 707, 845 and 846 squadrons in commission.
Notes: Capable of carrying up to 27 troops in the cabin or a wide variety of underslung loads up to 8,000lb in weight. 707 squadron is a training unit at RNAS YEOVILTON. 845 and 846 squadrons are based at YEOVILTON but able to embark or detach at short notice to support 3 Commando Brigade. The Sea King HC4 has a fixed undercarriage with no sponsons and no radome.

Westland LYNX

Variants: HAS 2, HAS 3
Roles: Surface search and strike; anti-submarine strike; SAR.
Engines: 2 x 900hp Rolls Royce GEM BS 360-07-26 free shaft turbines.
Rotor diameter: 42'0" **Length** 39'1¼" **Height** 11' 0" **Max Weight** 9,500lb.
Max Speed: 150 knots. **Crew**: 1 pilot and 1 observer.
Avionics: Ferranti SEA SPRAY radar. Marconi Orange Crop passive ESM equipment.
Armament: External pylons carry up to 4 x SEA SKUA air to surface missiles or 2 x STINGRAY, Mk 46 or Mk 44 torpedoes, depth charges, flares or markers.
Squadron Service: 702, 815 and 829 squadrons in commission.
Notes: 702 is a training squadron based at RNAS PORTLAND. 815, also based at Portland is the parent unit for single aircraft flights that embark in Type 42 destroyers and some classes of frigate, specialising in the surface strike role. 829 squadron parents flights in the Type 22 and other anti-submarine frigates. A version of the Lynx, the AH1, is operated by the Royal Marines Brigade Air Squadron which is based at RNAS Yeovilton and an improved naval version of the Lynx is undergoing development.
(HAS Mk 8) is now flying and undergoing intensive development trials.

Westland GAZELLE HT2

Engine: 1 x 592shp Turbomeca ASTAZOU free power turbine.
Crew: 1 or 2 pilots.
Notes: In service with 705 squadron at RNAS CULDROSE. Used for training all RN helicopter pilots up to "wings standard" before they move onto the SeaKing or Lynx. A version of the Gazelle, the AH1, is used by the Royal Marines Brigade Air Squadron based at RNAS Yeovilton.

OTHER AIRCRAFT TYPES IN ROYAL NAVY SERVICE DURING 1990/91

British Aerospace JETSTREAM T2 and T3
Engines: 2 x 940hp Turbomeca ASTAZOU 16D turboprops. (T3 Garrett turboprops).
Crew: 1 or 2 pilots, 2 student observers plus 3 other seats.
Notes: A number of these aircraft are used by 750 squadron at RNAS CULDROSE for training Fleet Air Arm Observers and also by the Heron flight at RNAS Yeovilton.

All Sea Devon and Sea Heron aircraft withdrawn from service in 1989.

de Havilland CHIPMUNK
Engine: 1 x 145hp de Havilland Gipsy Major 8 piston engine.
Crew: 2 pilots.
Notes: Used by the RN Flying Grading Flight at Roborough airport near Plymouth (and as such the first aircraft flown by generations of naval aircrew) and by stations flights at RNAS CULDROSE and YEOVILTON.

British Aerospace CANBERRA TT18

Engines: 2 x 6500lb thrust Rolls Royce AVON turbojets.
Crew: 1 pilot and 1 observer.
Notes: Used by the (civilian manned) Fleet Requirements and Aircraft Direction Unit (FRADU) at RNAS YEOVILTON. Canberras provide towed targets for live firings by ships at sea. Only 2 remain in service to be replaced by Falcon aircraft on contract to MOD(N).

Hawker HUNTER T8, GA11, T7 & T8m

Engine: 1 x 7575lb thrust Rolls Royce AVON turbojet.
Crew: T8 1 or 2 pilots. GA11 1 pilot. T7 1 or 2 pilots. T8m 1 or 2 pilots.
Notes: The Royal Navy has used Hunters to train fixed wing pilots since 1958. A number remain in service at RNAS YEOVILTON with the RN flying standards flight and with FRADU who use them as airborne targets for the aircraft direction school. 899 Squadron also use these aircraft as radar trainers for Sea Harrier pilots.

In addition to these aircraft, the following aircraft have naval functions:
CANBERRA T17: Used by 360 joint RN/RAF squadron for electronic warfare tasks. Based at RAF WYTON.
British Aerospace 125: Two aircraft, owned by the RN are operated by RN aircrew as part of 32 squadron RAF based at RAF NORTHOLT.
The Fleet Air Arm Historic flight based at RNAS YEOVILTON has a **SWORDFISH, SEAHAWK, FIREFLY and TIGER MOTH** on strength and these are often seen at air displays in the summer months.

Full details of these and many other naval aircraft can be found in the revised edition of AIRCRAFT OF THE ROYAL NAVY SINCE 1945 published by Maritime Books..

At the end of the line . . .

Readers may well find other warships afloat which are not mentioned in this book. The majority have fulfilled a long and useful life and are now relegated to non-seagoing duties. The following list gives details of their current duties:

Penn. No.	Ship	Remarks
C35	BELFAST	World War II Cruiser Museum ship—Pool of London (Open to the public)
D73	CAVALIER	World War II Destroyer. Museum Ship at Hebburn. Awaiting restoration.
D12	KENT	County Class Destroyer—Sea Cadet Training Ship at Portsmouth Future "under consideration"
F39	NAIAD	Static Trials Vessel—Portsmouth
F126	PLYMOUTH	Type 12 Frigate Museum Ship at Plymouth. Possible move to Gosport "under consideration".
S11	ORPHEUS	Oberon Class Submarine Harbour Training Ship at Gosport
S67	ALLIANCE	Submarine Museum Ship at Gosport (Open to the public)

At the time of publishing the following ships were awaiting tow for scrap or sale.

PORTSMOUTH	MILFORD HAVEN	ROSYTH	PLYMOUTH
Arethusa	Eskimo	Dreadnought	Aurora
Rame Head	Woodlark	Lofoten	Engadine (RFA)
Walkerton	(Targets)	Stalker	
Euryalus			

A number of merchant ships are on charter to various MOD departments. They include MAERSK ASCENSION, MAERSK GANNET, ST BRANDAN, INDOMITABLE, OIL MARINER & STENA SEASPREAD in support of the Falkland Island commitment. NORTHELLA, STARELLA and NORTHERN HORIZON have training/trials roles in UK waters.

NOTES

PHOTOGRAPHERS

The selection of photographs for use in the next edition will be made in October. We only use pictures of ships underway—preferably without a background. Please send SAE if you want photographs returned.